MW00533678

The Articles of Confederation Explained

THE LOCHLAINN SEABROOK COLLECTION

AMERICAN CIVIL WAR
Abraham Lincoln Was a Liberal, Jefferson Davis Was a Conservative: The Missing Key to Understanding the American Civil War
Confederacy 101: Amazing Facts You Never Knew About America's Oldest Political Tradition
Confederate Blood and Treasure: An Interview With Lochlainn Seabrook
Everything You Were Taught About African-Americans and the Civil War is Wrong, Ask a Southerner!
Everything You Were Taught About the Civil War is Wrong, Ask a Southerner!
Give This Book to a Yankee! A Southern Guide to the Civil War For Northerners
Heroes of the Southern Confederacy: The Illustrated Book of Confederate Officials, Soldiers, and Civilians
Lincoln's War: The Real Cause, the Real Winner, the Real Loser
The Great Yankee Coverup: What the North Doesn't Want You to Know About Lincoln's War!
The Ultimate Civil War Quiz Book: How Much Do You Really Know About America's Most Misunderstood Conflict?
Women in Gray: A Tribute to the Ladies Who Supported the Southern Confederacy

CONFEDERATE MONUMENTS
Confederate Monuments: Why Every American Should Honor Confederate Soldiers and Their Memorials

CONFEDERATE FLAG
Confederate Flag Facts: What Every American Should Know About Dixie's Southern Cross
What the Confederate Flag Means to Me: Americans Speak Out in Defense of Southern Honor, Heritage, and History

SECESSION
All We Ask Is To Be Let Alone: The Southern Secession Fact Book

SLAVERY
Everything You Were Taught About American Slavery is Wrong, Ask a Southerner!
Slavery 101: Amazing Facts You Never Knew About America's "Peculiar Institution"

CHILDREN
Honest Jeff and Dishonest Abe: A Southern Children's Guide to the Civil War
Saddle, Sword, and Gun: A Biography of Nathan Bedford Forrest For Teens

NATHAN BEDFORD FORREST
A Rebel Born: A Defense of Nathan Bedford Forrest - Confederate General, American Legend (winner of the 2011 Jefferson Davis Historical Gold Medal)
A Rebel Born: The Screenplay (film about N. B. Forrest)
Forrest! 99 Reasons to Love Nathan Bedford Forrest
Give 'Em Hell Boys! The Complete Military Correspondence of Nathan Bedford Forrest
I Rode With Forrest! Confederate Soldiers Who Served With the World's Greatest Cavalry Leader
Nathan Bedford Forrest and African-Americans: Yankee Myth, Confederate Fact
Nathan Bedford Forrest and the Battle of Fort Pillow: Yankee Myth, Confederate Fact
Nathan Bedford Forrest and the Ku Klux Klan: Yankee Myth, Confederate Fact
Nathan Bedford Forrest: Southern Hero, American Patriot - Honoring a Confederate Icon and the Old South
Saddle, Sword, and Gun: A Biography of Nathan Bedford Forrest For Teens
The God of War: Nathan Bedford Forrest As He Was Seen By His Contemporaries
The Quotable Nathan Bedford Forrest: Selections From the Writings and Speeches of the Confederacy's Most Brilliant Cavalryman

QUOTABLE SERIES
The Alexander H. Stephens Reader: Excerpts From the Works of a Confederate Founding Father
The Quotable Alexander H. Stephens: Selections From the Writings and Speeches of the Confederacy's First Vice President
The Quotable Jefferson Davis: Selections From the Writings and Speeches of the Confederacy's First President
The Quotable Nathan Bedford Forrest: Selections From the Writings and Speeches of the Confederacy's Most Brilliant Cavalryman
The Quotable Robert E. Lee: Selections From the Writings and Speeches of the South's Most Beloved Civil War General
The Quotable Stonewall Jackson: Selections From the Writings and Speeches of the South's Most Famous General
The Unquotable Abraham Lincoln: The President's Quotes They Don't Want You To Know!

CIVIL WAR BATTLES
Encyclopedia of the Battle of Franklin - A Comprehensive Guide to the Conflict that Changed the Civil War
Nathan Bedford Forrest and the Battle of Fort Pillow: Yankee Myth, Confederate Fact
The Battle of Franklin: Recollections of Confederate and Union Soldiers
The Battle of Nashville: Recollections of Confederate and Union Soldiers
The Battle of Spring Hill: Recollections of Confederate and Union Soldiers

CONSTITUTIONAL HISTORY
America's Three Constitutions: Complete Texts of the Articles of Confederation, Constitution of the United States of America, and Constitution of the Confederate States of America
The Articles of Confederation Explained: A Clause-by-Clause Study of America's First Constitution
The Constitution of the Confederate States of America Explained: A Clause-by-Clause Study of the South's Magna Carta

VICTORIAN CONFEDERATE LITERATURE
Rise Up and Call Them Blessed: Victorian Tributes to the Confederate Soldier, 1861-1901
Support Your Local Confederate: Wit and Humor in the Southern Confederacy
The God of War: Nathan Bedford Forrest As He Was Seen By His Contemporaries
The Old Rebel: Robert E. Lee As He Was Seen By His Contemporaries
Victorian Confederate Poetry: The Southern Cause in Verse, 1861-1901

ABRAHAM LINCOLN
Abraham Lincoln: The Southern View - Demythologizing America's Sixteenth President
Lincolnology: The Real Abraham Lincoln Revealed in His Own Words - A Study of Lincoln's Suppressed, Misinterpreted, and Forgotten Writings and Speeches
Lincoln's War: The Real Cause, the Real Winner, the Real Loser
The Great Impersonator! 99 Reasons to Dislike Abraham Lincoln
The Unholy Crusade: Lincoln's Legacy of Destruction in the American South
The Unquotable Abraham Lincoln: The President's Quotes They Don't Want You To Know!

NATURAL HISTORY
North America's Amazing Mammals: An Encyclopedia for the Whole Family
The Concise Book of Owls: A Guide to Nature's Most Mysterious Birds
The Concise Book of Tigers: A Guide to Nature's Most Remarkable Cats

PARANORMAL
Carnton Plantation Ghost Stories: True Tales of the Unexplained from Tennessee's Most Haunted Civil War House!
UFOs and Aliens: The Complete Guidebook

FAMILY HISTORIES
The Blakeneys: An Etymological, Ethnological, and Genealogical Study - Uncovering the Mysterious Origins of the Blakeney Family and Name
The Caudills: An Etymological, Ethnological, and Genealogical Study - Exploring the Name and National Origins of a European-American Family
The McGavocks of Carnton Plantation: A Southern History - Celebrating One of Dixie's Most Noble Confederate Families and Their Tennessee Home

MIND, BODY, SPIRIT
Autobiography of a Non-Yogi: A Scientist's Journey From Hinduism to Christianity (Dr. Amitava Dasgupta, with Lochlainn Seabrook)
Britannia Rules: Goddess-Worship in Ancient Anglo-Celtic Society - An Academic Look at the United Kingdom's Matricentric Spiritual Past
Christ Is All and In All: Rediscovering Your Divine Nature and the Kingdom Within
Christmas Before Christianity: How the Birthday of the "Sun" Became the Birthday of the "Son"
Jesus and the Gospel of Q: Christ's Pre-Christian Teachings As Recorded in the New Testament
Jesus and the Law of Attraction: The Bible-Based Guide to Creating Perfect Health, Wealth, and Happiness Following Christ's Simple Formula
Seabrook's Bible Dictionary of Traditional and Mystical Christian Doctrines
Sea Raven Press Blank Page Journal: For Reflections, Notes, and Sketches
The Bible and the Law of Attraction: 99 Teachings of Jesus, the Apostles, and the Prophets
The Book of Kelle: An Introduction to Goddess-Worship and the Great Celtic Mother-Goddess Kelle, Original Blessed Lady of Ireland
The Goddess Dictionary of Words and Phrases: Introducing a New Core Vocabulary for the Women's Spirituality Movement
Vintage Southern Cookbook: Delicious Dishes From Dixie

WOMEN
Aphrodite's Trade: The Hidden History of Prostitution Unveiled
Princess Diana: Modern Day Moon-Goddess - A Psychoanalytical and Mythological Look at Diana Spencer's Life, Marriage, and Death (with Dr. Jane Goldberg)
Women in Gray: A Tribute to the Ladies Who Supported the Southern Confederacy

REPRINTS
A Short History of the Confederate States of America (author Jefferson Davis; editor Lochlainn Seabrook)
Prison Life of Jefferson Davis (author John J. Craven; editor Lochlainn Seabrook)
Life of Beethoven (author Ludwig Nohl; editor Lochlainn Seabrook)
The New Revelation (author Arthur Conan Doyle; editor Lochlainn Seabrook)

Lochlainn Seabrook does not author books for fame and fortune, but for the love of writing and sharing his knowledge.

SeaRavenPress.com

Warning: SEA RAVEN PRESS BOOKS WILL EXPAND YOUR ★ MIND!

The Articles of Confederation

Explained

A Clause-by-Clause Study of America's First Constitution

★ Under the U.S. Confederacy 1781-1789 ★

THE COMPANION BOOK TO

The Constitution of the Confederate States of America Explained

Lochlainn Seabrook

AWARD-WINNING AUTHOR, HISTORIAN, & SCHOLAR

2014

SEA RAVEN PRESS, NASHVILLE, TENNESSEE, USA

THE ARTICLES OF CONFEDERATION EXPLAINED

Published by
Sea Raven Press, Cassidy Ravensdale, President
Nashville, Tennessee, USA
SeaRavenPress.com • searavenpress@gmail.com

SEA RAVEN PRESS
REVOLUTIONARY BOOKS FOR HISTORY LOVERS!

Copyright © text and illustrations Lochlainn Seabrook 2014, 2019, 2020, 2021 in accordance with U.S. and international copyright laws and regulations, as stated and protected under the Berne Union for the Protection of Literary and Artistic Property (Berne Convention), and the Universal Copyright Convention (the UCC). All rights reserved under the Pan-American and International Copyright Conventions.

PRINTING HISTORY
• 1st SRP paperback ed., 1st printing, January 2014; 1st ed., 2nd printing, July 2019; 1st ed., 3rd printing, October 2020; 1st ed. 4th printing, November 2021, ISBN: 978-0-9858632-8-9
• 1st SRP hardcover ed., 1st printing, November 2021, ISBN: 978-1-955351-12-6

ISBN: 978-1-955351-12-6 (hardcover)
Library of Congress Control Number: 2021950890

This work is the copyrighted intellectual property of Lochlainn Seabrook and has been registered with the Copyright Office at the Library of Congress in Washington, D.C., USA. No part of this work (including text, covers, drawings, photos, illustrations, maps, images, diagrams, etc.), in whole or in part, may be used, reproduced, stored in a retrieval system, or transmitted, in any form or by any means now known or hereafter invented, without written permission from the publisher. The sale, duplication, hire, lending, copying, digitalization, or reproduction of this material, in any manner or form whatsoever, is also prohibited, and is a violation of federal, civil, and digital copyright law, which provides severe civil and criminal penalties for any violations.

The Articles of Confederation Explained: A Clause-by-Clause Study of America's First Constitution, by Lochlainn Seabrook. Includes an introduction, appendix, and bibliography.

Front and back cover design and art, book design, layout, and interior art by Lochlainn Seabrook.
All images, image captions, graphic design, & graphic art copyright © Lochlainn Seabrook.
All images selected, placed, manipulated, cleaned, colored, tinted, and/or created by Lochlainn Seabrook.
Cover image: George Washington presiding at the Constitutional Convention 1787, engraving by John Rogers.

All persons who approve of the authority and principles of Colonel Lochlainn Seabrook's literary work, and realize its benefits as a means of reeducating the world concerning the truth about American history, are hereby requested to avidly recommend his books to others and to vigorously cooperate in extending their reach, scope, and influence around the globe.

The views on the American "Civil War" documented in this book are those of the publisher.

WRITTEN, PUBLISHED, PRINTED, & MANUFACTURED IN THE UNITED STATES OF AMERICA

SEA RAVEN PRESS

Dedication

To the valiant and sagacious Conservative men and women who intended the United States to be a confederacy, formed it as a "Confederate Republic," called it "the Confederacy," nicknamed it "the Confederate States of America," and designated our first constitution the "Articles of Confederation." May their memories and ideals live perpetually in the hearts of true patriots everywhere.

Epigraph

"[I am] extremely uneasy at the proposed change of government . . . If a wrong step be made now, the republic may be lost forever. If this new government will not come up to the expectation of the people, and they shall be disappointed, their liberty will be lost, and tyranny must and will arise. . . . I am sure [that my liberal colleagues are] fully impressed with the necessity of forming a great consolidated government, instead of a confederation. That this is a consolidated [big] government is demonstrably clear; and

Patrick Henry

the danger of such a government is, to my mind, very striking. . . . Who authorized them to speak the language of, *We, the people*, instead of *We, the states*? States are the characteristics and the soul of a confederation. If the states be not the agents of this compact, it must be one great, consolidated, national government, of the people of all the states. . . . The Confederation, this same despised government, merits, in my opinion, the highest encomium: it carried us through a long and dangerous war; it rendered us victorious in that bloody conflict with a powerful nation; it has secured us a territory greater than any European monarch possesses: and shall a government which has been thus strong and vigorous, be accused of imbecility, and abandoned for want of energy? Consider what you are about to do before you part with the [Confederate] government. Take longer time in reckoning things; revolutions like this have happened in almost every country in Europe; similar examples are to be found in ancient Greece and ancient Rome—instances of the people losing their liberty by their own carelessness and the ambition of a few. We are cautioned by the honorable gentleman [Edmund Pendleton], who presides, against faction and turbulence. I acknowledge that licentiousness is dangerous, and that it ought to be provided against: I acknowledge, also, [that] the new [federal] form of government may effectually prevent it: yet there is another thing it will as effectually do—it will oppress and ruin the people. . . . I am not well versed in history, but I will submit to your recollection whether liberty has been destroyed most often by the licentiousness of the people or by the tyranny of rulers? I imagine, sir, you will find the balance on the side of tyranny. Happy will you be if you miss the fate of those nations, who, omitting to resist their oppressors, or negligently suffering their liberty to be wrested from them, have groaned under intolerable despotism!"

in debate at the June 4, 1788, convention at Richmond, Virginia, concerning discarding both the Articles of Confederation and the Confederacy in order to replace them with the new U.S. Constitution and strong central government.

Contents

SEA RAVEN PRESS
—INSPIRING BOOKS—
For the Whole Family
SeaRavenPress.com
NASHVILLE, TENNESSEE

Notes to the Reader

☛ Modern transcriptions of the Articles of Confederation are not particularly precise, and the original documents are difficult to decipher due to age and fading. Nonetheless I have used what I consider to be the most accurate reading of the Articles.

☛ For the sake of posterity I have retained the 18th-Century spellings, punctuation, wording, and formatting of the original articles.

☛ As they share the same meaning, throughout this book I use the words "clause" and "article" interchangeably.

☛ Brackets within quotes and clauses contain my comments, clarifications, and corrections.

☛ In any study of early American history it is vitally important to keep in mind that in 1860 the platforms of the two major political parties were the opposite of what they are today. In other words, the Democrats of the mid 19th Century were Conservatives, akin to the Republican Party of today, while the Republicans of the mid 19th Century were Liberals, akin to the Democratic Party of today. The Democrats would not become left-leaning and the Republicans would not become right-leaning until the election of 1896. For an in-depth discussion on this topic see my book, *Abraham Lincoln Was a Liberal, Jefferson Davis Was a Conservative: The Missing Key to Understanding the American Civil War.*

Introduction

A Brief History of the
Articles of Confederation

by Lochlainn Seabrook

he Declaration of Independence of 1776 severed all ties with the English government that had formally guided, governed, and protected the original thirteen American colonies. Realizing that some type of new social control was now needed, the colonists began to look at the idea of self-government. And yet, after years under a ruthless and corrupt British monarchy, most had become extremely mistrustful of any type of polity.

The solution was soon in coming. Between 1777 and 1780 the American colonists began setting up their own individual state constitutions, many which included a Bill of Rights that placed limitations on their individual governments. In great measure these first attempts at self-government were predicated on the principle of John Locke's concept of "natural rights," which asserts that humanity, being born free and independent, possesses the inherent God-given "natural rights of life, liberty, and property."

To insure the maintenance of these natural rights, the colonists decided that they would set up the American government specifically as a *confederacy*, or what Thomas Jefferson called a "Confederate Republic": a body of states united to form a loose "association" in which the states retain all sovereign power, while the central government is legally dependent on the will of the states. As a result, the concept of confederation became so deeply ingrained in the American psyche that the U.S. was, in fact, officially called "the Confederacy," not just between 1781 and 1789, but right up to the time of the War for Southern Independence in 1861. Revealingly, from the very beginning, the fledgling U.S. was nicknamed "the Confederate States of America" by both Americans and foreigners.

Though libertarian and conservative minded individuals (known then as "Federalists") believed that these first state governments successfully represented the people, the liberal among the populace (known then as "Nationalists") felt strongly that a central government was needed to oversee the entire Confederacy. They felt, for example, that since it had no clearly defined or official authority by which to administrate, the Continental Congress was entirely powerless to effect real and lasting change, for its sole legal power came from the states, which was voluntary.

Thus, in 1776 the Continental Congress put forth the idea of the "Articles of Confederation," in essence, an effort to create a type of national government through more fully empowering Congress itself. This idea was popular, in part, because such a government would help ensure an American win in the Revolutionary War. But there was also a need for the peacetime defense of national borders, engaging in foreign relations, and establishing a universal postal system, none of which the individual states had the ability to either implement or manage.

On June 11, 1776, a congressional committee, led by John Dickinson of Delaware, was formed to write up the articles. With one representative from each state (or colony), the committee intended to create a confederacy that would provide the states with congressional representation based on population, while giving to the federal government those powers that had not been assigned to the states.

Intense debate, lasting many months, ensued, essentially pitting what we now call Conservatives (those for small limited government) against Liberals (those for large unlimited government). The end product was one that pleased few but appeased most—at least temporarily.

The Articles of Confederation gave each state one vote in Congress, and allowed the states control over all law enforcement and judicial proceedings within their borders. The central government, in turn, was authorized to declare war, raise an army and navy, strike coinage, establish weights and measures, make foreign treaties, and oversee Native American affairs, though it was prohibited from directly taxing the states.

John Dickinson

By stipulating that the states were allowed to keep every power "which is not by this confederation expressly delegated to the United States," the new confederacy avoided the colonists' worst fear: the formation of a *nation*, with all of its autocratic, dictatorial overtones and terrible memories of monarchical English rule. In place of a nation, they very intentionally chose to form a "firm league of friendship" with one another.

Congress adopted the Articles of Confederation on November 15, 1777, but due to numerous delays they were not officially formalized until Maryland's ratification of the document on March 1, 1781 (the last state to do so). It was on this day that the Continental Congress became the Confederate Congress, and the union of our first "Confederate States of America" was born. Between the years 1779 and 1789, ten men, beginning with Samuel Huntington of Connecticut, would serve as president of this, our original Confederate Republic (see Appendix).

Though the Revolutionary War came to an end only a few months later, the new Confederate Congress found itself with plenty of other issues to deal with. Chief among these was what to do with the great unnamed Western Territories. This problem was resolved by the Ordinances of 1784, 1785, and 1787, which divided, surveyed, and organized these lands into what would later become America's Western and Northwestern states.

Rigorous libertarian and conservative minded colonists, of course, loved the new U.S. Confederacy, with its small, almost invisible and nearly powerless central government. Fearing centralization of any kind, or what they called "consolidation," they enjoyed the immense political freedom and individual liberties granted to them under the Articles of Confederation, and which, at the same time, prevented Congress from meddling in their personal and state affairs.

But these individuals were in the minority, and no sooner had the ink dried on the parchment than the Liberal minded majority (the Nationalists) began to complain about everything the Conservatives (the Federalists) liked about the Articles of Confederation.

For one thing, the Nationalists argued, the articles gave Congress no power to enforce law or regulate foreign trade. Worse still, Congress could not levy state taxes. Instead, it had to ask, and in many cases literally beg, the states for money, the result being that Congress could not control the public debt. Lastly, they held, without a judiciary or an official president, the central government, rendered virtually "ineffective" by the articles, was unable to interpret laws, regulate commerce, or carry out the acts of Congress.

By 1787 the tide had turned against the idea of a strictly confederated United States of America, and a constitutional convention was commenced in Philadelphia, Pennsylvania, on May 14 of that year with the idea of amending the Articles of Confederation. One of those who presided at the notable event was future U.S. president George Washington (see the cover of this book).

After much wrangling and debate, however, it was apparent that what the majority actually wanted was not to simply improve the articles. They desired an entirely new form of polity, one with an all-powerful, consolidated central government that had authority over the legislatures of the individual states. The main idea put forward was that of a "supreme power," one that would simultaneously destroy the concept of state sovereignty. In other words, they wanted a nationalized government, what we now call "big government."

There were sporadic revolts against the plan to strongly centralize the government, but with the tempering voices of Thomas Jefferson, John Jay, John Adams, and Patrick Henry (who famously said "I smell a rat") absent from the proceedings (for various reasons), the U.S. Confederacy had little hope of surviving intact.

The unavoidable result of the Philadelphia Convention was a new governing document: the U.S. Constitution, our second constitution, and the simultaneous birth of the United States as a nation-like constitutional republic.

Adopted on September 17, 1787, ratified on June 21, 1788, and made effective on March 4, 1789, the establishment of the new federal government and the U.S. Constitution marked the formal end of the American Confederacy. Officially, it had lasted only eight short years, from 1781 to 1789.

But the flame of confederalism (also known as conservatism, Americanism, antifederalism, or Jeffersonianism—after Thomas Jefferson) was not extinguished in 1789. It merely went underground, resurfacing seventy-one years later in 1860, with the election of big government Liberal Abraham Lincoln on November 6. (Note: The two major parties were reversed in the 1860s, and would not become the parties we know today until the election of 1896.) It was only a few weeks afterward, on December 20, that, following the example of the original thirteen colonies who broke from the tyranny of Great Britain, the first of eleven Southern states (and portions of two others, making thirteen in all) began to secede in an effort to flee the tyranny of the Liberal-run Union.

At the very foundation of the Southern secession movement was the desire to preserve the Conservative ideals of the original Confederate Founding Fathers of 1781, which were embedded in America's first constitution, the Articles of Confederation. And so the new republic gave itself a name that would honor both their politically conservative ancestors and the form of government that they loved and cherished: the Confederacy, or more formally, "the Confederate States of America" (C.S.A.).

By repeatedly violating the U.S. Constitution and ignoring both American and international law, progressive Lincoln—who was, of course, enthusiastically supported by socialists (such as Karl Marx) both inside and outside his administration—was able to "put down the rebellion" in just four years.

But once again, the idea of the Confederacy, of a restricted confederated government, did not simply die out with the Conservative Robert E. Lee's capitulation to the Liberal Ulysses S. Grant on April 9, 1865. The confederate ideals of our colonial forefathers—that of natural rights, personal liberty, state sovereignty, and limited government—live on today in the hearts of authentic Conservatives and Libertarians everywhere.

As a Conservative myself, and a cousin of arch confederalist Patrick Henry, it is my hope that this booklet will continue to help keep the light of the Confederacy alive, and inspire future generations to energetically protect their liberties. If they do not, the causes for which our courageous sires fought both the first Revolutionary War and the second Revolutionary War (the so-called "Civil War"), will be forever lost: personal freedom and self-government.

DON'T TREAD ON ME

Lochlainn Seabrook
Nashville, Tennessee, USA
January 2014

The
Articles of Confederation
Explained

A Clause-by-Clause Study of
America's First Constitution

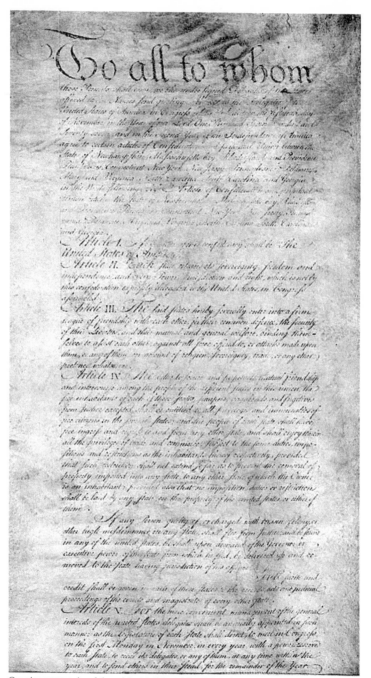

Opening paragraphs of the original Articles of Confederation, showing Articles 1 through 5.

Articles of Confederation

and

Perpetual Union Between the States

November 15, 1777

TO ALL TO WHOM these Presents shall come, we, the undersigned Delegates of the States affixed to our Names, send greeting.

Whereas the Delegates of the United States of America, in Congress assembled, did, on the fifteenth day of November in the Year of our Lord One Thousand Seven Hundred and Seventy Seven, and in the Second Year of the Independence of America, agree to certain articles of Confederation and perpetual Union between the States of Newhampshire, Massachusetts-bay, Rhodeisland and Providence Plantations, Connecticut, New-York, New-Jersey, Pennsylvania, Delaware, Maryland, Virginia, North-Carolina, South-Carolina, and Georgia, in the words following, viz. *Articles of Confederation and perpetual Union between the states of Newhampshire, Massachusetts-bay, Rhodeisland and Providence Plantations, Connecticut, New-York, New-Jersey, Pennsylvania, Delaware, Maryland, Virginia, North-carolina, South-carolina, and Georgia.*

EXPLANATION: The opening paragraphs record the date, the thirteen states that are involved in the creation and ratification of the Articles of Confederation, and the intention of the Constitution: to form a "perpetual union" between said states.

Note, that by the word "perpetual" it is not intended to mean that a state cannot leave (secede from) the Confederacy. Merely that the union itself will continue indefinitely, regardless of how many states decide to join or leave. Indeed, under the U.S. Constitution secession has always been a legal states' right (see the 9th and 10th Amendments).

Article 1

The Stile of this Confederacy shall be "The United States of America."

EXPLANATION: This clause sets forth and establishes the name ("style") of the new American Confederacy: "The United States of America."

Arthur St. Clair, ninth President of the U.S. Confederacy.

Article 2

Each State retains its sovereignty, freedom, and independence, and every Power, Jurisdiction and right, which is not by this confederation expressly delegated to the United States, in congress assembled.

EXPLANATION: This clause affirms that after joining the U.S. Confederacy, the individual states will hold onto their rights of self-rule, self-government, and self-determination, while maintaining complete independence from the central government. The only exceptions to this are those powers and rights that are granted to the Confederate Congress. Note: Article 2 became the 10th Amendment in the U.S. Constitution's Bill of Rights, where the limiting (i.e., conservative) word "expressly" was removed.

Article 3

The said states hereby severally [i.e., separately and independently] enter into a firm league of friendship with each other, for their common defence, the security of their Liberties, and their mutual and general welfare, binding themselves to assist each other, against all force offered to, or attacks made upon them, or any of them, on account of religion, sovereignty, trade, or any other pretence whatever.

EXPLANATION: In this clause the Confederate delegation makes it clear that the new Confederacy is not a nation, but rather a "league of friendship" between wholly sovereign nation-states. Within this league the individual nation-states are expected to join forces in the case of foreign attack on their soil, their rights, and their "general welfare" due to religious reasons, commercial ventures, their political independence, or for any other reason.

Article 4

The better to secure and perpetuate mutual friendship and intercourse among the people of the different states in this union, the free inhabitants of each of these states, paupers, vagabonds and fugitives from Justice excepted, shall be entitled to all privileges and immunities of free citizens in the several states; and the people of each state shall have free ingress and regress to and from any other state, and shall enjoy therein all the privileges of trade and commerce, subject to the same duties, impositions [i.e., penalties or taxes] and restrictions as the inhabitants thereof respectively, provided that such restrictions shall not extend so far as to prevent the removal of property imported into any state, to any other state of which the Owner is an inhabitant; provided also that no imposition, duties or restriction shall be laid by any state, on the property of the united states, or either of them.

If any Person guilty of, or charged with treason, felony, or other high misdemeanor in any state, shall flee from Justice, and be found in any of the united states, he shall upon demand of the Governor or executive power, of the state from which he fled, be delivered up and removed to the state having jurisdiction of his offence.

Full faith and credit shall be given in each of these states to the records, acts and judicial proceedings of the courts and magistrates of every other state.

EXPLANATION: In order to protect and maintain the "league of friendship" between the states, this clause—which became Article 4, Sections 1 through 4, of the U.S. Constitution—establishes equal rights to U.S. citizens across all thirteen states, allowing free and open travel between states, giving each citizen the same rights as the inhabitants of the state they happen to be in.

At the same time, it also imposes the individual laws of each state on the traveler, such as that state's taxes, importation rules, etc.

The exceptions to this article are the indigent, the homeless, criminals, and fugitives. In these cases such individuals must be sent back to their original home state.

Finally, each state must honor the laws of its fellow states.

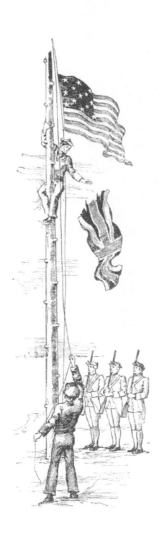

Article 5

For the more convenient management of the general interests of the united states, delegates shall be annually appointed in such manner as the legislature of each state shall direct, to meet in congress on the first Monday in November, in every year, with a power reserved to each state, to recall its delegates, or any of them, at any time within the year, and to send others in their stead, for the remainder of the Year.

No state shall be represented in congress by less than two, nor by more than seven Members; and no person shall be capable of being a delegate for more than three years in any term of six years; nor shall any person, being a delegate, be capable of holding any office under the united states, for which he, or another for his benefit receives any salary, fees or emolument of any kind.

Each state shall maintain its own delegates in a meeting of the states, and while they act as members of the committee of the states.

In determining questions in the united states, in congress assembled, each state shall have one vote.

Freedom of speech and debate in congress shall not be impeached or questioned in any Court, or place out of congress, and the members of congress shall be protected in their persons from arrests and imprisonments, during the time of their going to and from, and attendance on congress, except for treason, felony, or breach of the peace.

EXPLANATION: To aid in the efficient management of the Confederacy, this clause stipulates that Congressional members are to be appointed by their state legislatures (in 1913 this rule was overturned by the 17th Amendment, Clause 1, which calls for senators to be elected by popular not legislative vote), that the states will meet in Congress on the first Monday of November each year, and that the states have the power to send or recall any delegate they like.

Each state is allowed a congressional delegation of from two to seven individuals, delegates cannot serve for more than three years during any term of six years (i.e., simultaneous holding of more than one office is prohibited, a rule that served as the model for the "separation of powers" concept in the U.S. Constitution), and a delegate cannot hold any U.S. office in which he is paid by wage, gifts, or rewards of any kind.

The states are in charge of financially supporting their own delegates, and each state has one vote in the Confederate Congress.

Congressmen have freedom of speech, both in and out of Congress, and may not be questioned, impeached, arrested, or imprisoned, except for treason, committing a felony, or disturbing the peace. This particular rule was carried over to the U.S. Constitution as Article 1, Section 6, Clause 1.

Article 6

No state without the Consent of the united states in congress assembled, shall send any embassy to, or receive any embassy from, or enter into any conference, agreement, alliance or treaty with any King, prince or state; nor shall any person holding any office of profit or trust under the united states, or any of them, accept of any present, emolument, office or title of any kind whatever, from any king, prince or foreign state; nor shall the united states in congress assembled, or any of them, grant any title of nobility.

No two or more states shall enter into any treaty, confederation or alliance whatever between them, without the consent of the united states in congress assembled, specifying accurately the purposes for which the same is to be entered into, and how long it shall continue.

No state shall lay any imposts or duties, which may interfere with any stipulations in treaties, entered into by the united states in congress assembled, with any king, prince or state, in pursuance of any treaties already proposed by congress, to the courts of France and Spain.

No vessels of war shall be kept up in time of peace by any state, except such number only, as shall be deemed necessary by the united states in congress assembled, for the defence of such state, or its trade; nor shall any body of forces be kept up by any state, in time of peace, except such number only, as in the judgment of the united states, in congress assembled, shall be deemed requisite to garrison the forts necessary for the defence of such state; but every state shall always keep up a well regulated and disciplined militia, sufficiently armed and accoutred, and shall provide and have constantly ready for use, in public stores, a due number of field pieces and tents, and a proper quantity of arms, ammunition and camp equipage.

No state shall engage in any war without the consent of the united states in congress assembled, unless such state be actually invaded by enemies, or shall have received certain advice of a resolution being formed by some nation of Indians to invade such state, and the danger is so imminent as not to admit of a delay, till the united states in congress assembled can be consulted; nor shall any state grant commissions to any ships or vessels of war, nor letters of marque or reprisal, except it be after a declaration of war by the united states in congress assembled, and then only against the kingdom or state and the subjects thereof, against which war has been so declared, and under such regulations as shall be established by the united states in congress assembled, unless such state be infested by pirates, in which case vessels of was may be fitted out for that occasion, and kept so long as the danger shall continue, or until the united states in congress assembled, shall determine otherwise.

EXPLANATION: This clause—which was later absorbed into both the United States Constitution (1787) and the Confederate States Constitution (1861) as Article 1, Section 10, Clauses 1 through 3—lays out the limitations on the powers of the thirteen states, while describing the powers of the central Confederate government.

To begin with, the states cannot send ambassadors to or receive ambassadors from royals or foreign states, nor can they form agreements or partnerships with them. No U.S. office holder can accept gifts, profit from, or receive offices or titles from any royal or foreign state. Neither the states or the Confederate Congress are allowed to give out noble titles.

The Confederate states are not allowed to form agreements or partnerships with other states in the Confederacy, unless they have been given permission to do so by the Confederate Congress. Even then, states wishing to form such coalitions must have good reason for desiring them, and must give a full account of the purpose and duration of the alliance.

The states cannot create taxes that conflict with current treaties or future treaties with France of Spain. The states are also prohibited from maintaining navies or standing armies, unless considered necessary by the Confederate Congress. However, the individual states are ordered to establish "a well regulated and disciplined militia," complete with arms, ammunition, and camp and field supplies.

This particular clause also declares it illegal for a state to engage in war without the express permission of Congress, unless an invasion by foreigners or Native Americans is imminent. States are also barred from commissioning war ships, unless Congress has declared war or the state has been "infested by pirates."

In short, only the Confederate Congress is permitted to engage in political, commercial, foreign relations or declare war.

Article 7

When land-forces are raised by any state for the common defence, all officers of or under the rank of colonel, shall be appointed by the legislature of each state respectively, by whom such forces shall be raised, or in such manner as such state shall direct, and all vacancies shall be filled up by the state which first made the appointment.

EXPLANATION: This clause announces that if and when Congress declares war and armies are raised to defend the Confederacy, that the individual state legislatures must appoint colonels and all ranks below colonel.

Article 8

All charges of war, and all other expenses that shall be incurred for the common defence or general welfare, and allowed by the united states in congress assembled, shall be defrayed out of a common treasury, which shall be supplied by the several states, in proportion to the value of all land within each state, granted to or surveyed for any Person, as such land and the buildings and improvements thereon shall be estimated according to such mode as the united states in congress assembled, shall from time to time, direct and appoint.

The taxes for paying that proportion shall be laid and levied by the authority and direction of the legislatures of the several states within the time agreed upon by the united states in congress assembled.

EXPLANATION: In this clause the U.S. Confederacy orders that the costs of warfare will be raised and paid through a common state treasury, each state contributing in proportion to the value of its land. The state legislatures are to oversee payment according to a time schedule created by Congress.

John Penn of North Carolina, signatory.

Article 9

The united states in congress assembled, shall have the sole and exclusive right and power of determining on peace and war, except in the cases mentioned in the sixth article—of sending and receiving ambassadors—entering into treaties and alliances, provided that no treaty of commerce shall be made whereby the legislative power of the respective states shall be restrained from imposing such imposts and duties on foreigners, as their own people are subjected to, or from prohibiting the exportation or importation of any species of goods or commodities whatsoever—of establishing rules for deciding in all cases, what captures on land or water shall be legal, and in what manner prizes taken by land or naval forces in the service of the united states shall be divided or appropriated—of granting letters of marque and reprisal in times of peace—appointing courts for the trial of piracies and felonies committed on the high seas and establishing courts for receiving and determining finally appeals in all cases of captures, provided that no member of congress shall be appointed a judge of any of the said courts.

The united states in congress assembled shall also be the last resort on appeal in all disputes and differences now subsisting or that hereafter may arise between two or more states concerning boundary, jurisdiction or any other cause whatever; which authority shall always be exercised in the manner following. Whenever the legislative or executive authority or lawful agent of any state in controversy with another shall present a petition to congress, stating the matter in question and praying for a hearing, notice thereof shall be given by order of congress to the legislative or executive authority of the other state in controversy, and a day assigned for the appearance of the parties by their lawful agents, who shall then be directed to appoint by joint consent, commissioners or judges to constitute a court for hearing and determining the matter in question: but if they cannot agree, congress shall name three persons out of each of the united states, and from the list of such persons each party shall alternately strike out one, the petitioners beginning, until the number shall be reduced to thirteen; and from that number not less than seven, nor more than nine names as congress shall direct, shall in the presence of congress be drawn out by lot, and the persons whose names shall be so drawn or any five of them, shall be commissioners or judges, to hear and finally determine the controversy, so always as a major part of the judges who shall hear the cause shall agree in the determination: and if either party shall neglect to attend at the day appointed, without showing reasons, which congress shall judge sufficient, or being present shall refuse to strike, the congress shall proceed to nominate three persons out of each state, and the secretary of congress shall strike in behalf of such party absent or refusing; and the judgment and sentence of the court to be appointed, in the manner before prescribed, shall be final and conclusive; and if any of the parties shall refuse to submit to the authority of such court, or to appear or defend their claim or cause, the court shall nevertheless proceed to pronounce sentence, or judgment, which shall in like manner be final and decisive, the judgment or sentence and other proceedings being in either case transmitted to congress, and lodged among the acts of congress for the security of the parties concerned: provided that every commissioner, before he sits in judgment, shall take an oath to be administered by one of the judges of the supreme or superior court of the state, where the cause shall be tried, "well and truly to hear and determine the matter in question, according to the best of his judgment, without favour, affection or hope of reward:" provided also that no state shall be deprived of territory for the benefit of the united states.

All controversies concerning the private right of soil claimed under different grants of two or more states, whose jurisdictions as they may respect such lands, and the states which passed such grants are adjusted, the said grants or either of them being at the same time claimed to have originated antecedent to such settlement of jurisdiction, shall on the petition of either party to the congress of the united states, be finally determined as near as may be in the same manner as is before prescribed for deciding disputes respecting territorial jurisdiction between different states.

The united states in congress assembled shall also have the sole and exclusive right and power of regulating the alloy and value of coin struck by their own authority, or by that of the respective states—fixing the standard of weights and measures throughout the United States—regulating the trade and managing all affairs with the Indians, not members of any of the states, provided that the legislative right of any state within its own limits be not infringed or violated—establishing or regulating post-offices from one state to another, throughout all the united states, and exacting such postage on the papers passing thro' the same as may be requisite to defray the expenses of the said office—appointing all officers of the land forces, in the service of the united states, excepting regimental officers—appointing all the officers of the naval forces, and commissioning all officers whatever in the service of the united states—making rules for the government and regulation of the said land and naval forces, and directing their operations.

The united states in congress assembled shall have authority to appoint a committee, to sit in the recess of congress, to be denominated "A Committee of the States," and to consist of one delegate from each state; and to appoint such other committees and civil officers as may be necessary for managing the general affairs of the united states under their direction—to appoint one of their number to preside, provided that no person be allowed to serve in the office of president more than one year in any term of three years; to ascertain the necessary sums of money to be raised for the service of the united states, and to appropriate and apply the same for defraying the public expenses—to borrow money, or emit bills [i.e., print money] on the credit of the united states, transmitting every half year to the respective states an account of the sums of money so borrowed or emitted,—to build and equip a navy—to agree upon the number of land forces, and to make requisitions from each state for its quota, in proportion to the number of white inhabitants in such state; which requisition shall be binding, and thereupon the legislature of each state shall appoint the regimental officers, raise the men and cloath, arm and equip them in a soldier like manner, at the expense of the united states; and the officers and men so cloathed, armed and equipped shall march to the place appointed, and within the time agreed on by the united states in congress assembled: But if the united states in congress assembled shall, on consideration of circumstances judge proper that any state should not raise men, or should raise a smaller number than its quota, and that any other state should raise a greater number of men than the quota thereof, such extra number shall be raised, officered, clothed, armed and equipped in the same manner as the quota of such state, unless the legislature of such state shall judge that such extra number cannot be safely spared out of the same, in which case they shall raise officer, cloath, arm and equip as many of such extra number as they judge can be safely spared. And the officers and men so cloathed, armed and equipped, shall march to the place appointed, and within the time agreed on by the united states in congress assembled.

The united states in congress assembled shall never engage in a war, nor grant letters of marque and reprisal in time of peace, nor enter into any treaties or alliances, nor coin money, nor regulate the value thereof, nor ascertain the sums and expenses necessary for the defence and welfare of the united states, or any of them, nor emit bills, nor borrow money on the credit of the united states, nor appropriate money, nor agree upon the number of vessels of war, to be built or purchased, or the number of land or sea forces to be raised, nor appoint a commander in chief of the army or navy, unless nine states assent to the same: nor shall a question on any other point, except for adjourning from day to day be determined, unless by the votes of a majority of the united states in congress assembled.

The congress of the united states shall have power to adjourn to any time within the year, and to any place within the united states, so that no period of adjournment be for a longer duration than the space of six months, and shall publish the Journal of their proceedings monthly, except such parts thereof relating to treaties, alliances or military operations, as in their judgment require secrecy; and the yeas and nays of the delegates of each state on any question shall be entered on the Journal, when it is desired by any delegate; and the delegates of a state, or any of them, at his or their request shall be furnished with a transcript of the said Journal, except such parts as are above accepted, to lay before the legislatures of the several states.

EXPLANATION: This clause lays out the powers of the central government, that is, the Confederate Congress, beginning with its sole right to declare war, send and receive ambassadors, enter into agreements and partnerships, decide how the spoils of war are to be dealt with, issue letters of marque and reprisal (that is, authorizing privateers), and set up courts to handle piracy and other crimes "on the high seas."

A state that finds itself in dispute with another state can appeal to Congress as a last resort. If necessary, Congress will appoint between seven and nine individuals to act as judges, whose decision on the case will be final.

The Confederate Congress has the sole power to fix weights and measures, determine the value of money, and regulate trade and all other issues with Native Americans living outside official U.S. boundaries. It also has the right to set up and operate post offices throughout the states, issue postage stamps, establish rules for the central government, the army, and the navy, and appoint all U.S. army and navy officers (except regimental officers).

When Congress is in recess, it has the right to appoint an interim executive committee called "A Committee of the States," made up of one delegate from each state. Only Congress has the right to borrow money, decide the amount of money needed by Congress (and how to portion it out), and set up and equip an army and navy based on the number of white inhabitants per state.

While the U.S. Confederacy had no official president in the modern sense, the articles provide for a "president" to preside over the Confederate Congress, to be appointed from among the delegates to serve for a period of not "more than one year in any term of three years."

Finally, the Confederate Congress cannot act on any of these rights without the consent of at least nine of the thirteen states, though it does have the power to adjourn at any time of the year for up to six months. Congress is required to publish a monthly journal of its proceedings, but need not reveal anything deemed "secret." Delegates can request a transcript of the congressional journal for their state legislatures.

Article 10

The committee of the states, or any nine of them, shall be authorized to execute, in the recess of congress, such of the powers of congress as the united states in congress assembled, by the consent of nine states, shall from time to time think expedient to vest them with; provided that no power be delegated to the said committee, for the exercise of which, by the articles of confederation, the voice of nine states in the congress of the united states assembled is requisite.

EXPLANATION: In this clause the U.S. Confederacy defines the powers of the "Committee of the States," which goes into operation while Congress is in recess. The committee has the same powers as Congress (laid out in Article 9), and can execute congressional laws as it sees fit, but only if nine of the thirteen states agree by vote.

Article 11

Canada acceding to this confederation, and joining in the measures of the united states, shall be admitted into, and entitled to all the advantages of this union: but no other colony shall be admitted into the same, unless such admission be agreed to by nine states.

EXPLANATION: This clause preapproves Canada's (that is, Quebec's) admittance into the U.S. Confederacy (if it so desires), with all of the same rights as the original thirteen states. However, other American colonies wishing to join the union need the approval of nine states.

Article 12

All bills of credit emitted, monies borrowed and debts contracted by, or under the authority of congress, before the assembling of the united states, in pursuance of the present confederation, shall be deemed and considered as a charge against the united states, for payment and satisfaction whereof the said united states, and the public faith are hereby solemnly pledged.

EXPLANATION: This clause states that the "present confederation" will be responsible for any and all debts incurred by the Confederate Congress prior to the creation and signing of the Articles of Confederation.

Article 13

Every state shall abide by the determinations of the united states in congress assembled, on all questions which by this confederation is submitted to them. And the Articles of this confederation shall be inviolably observed by every state, and the union shall be perpetual; nor shall any alteration at any time hereafter be made in any of them; unless such alteration be agreed to in a congress of the united states, and be afterwards confirmed by the legislatures of every state.

EXPLANATION: This clause affirms that the states must obey all of the laws set up by the Confederate Congress, additionally stipulating that the Articles of Confederation are meant to be "perpetual." Changes, that is amendments, to this constitution can only be made by Congress, and with the approval of all thirteen states, a tradition adopted from the various state constitutions.

Signatories

And whereas it hath pleased the Great Governor of the World [God] to incline the hearts of the legislatures we respectively represent in congress, to approve of, and to authorize us to ratify the said articles of confederation and perpetual union. Know Ye that we the undersigned delegates, by virtue of the power and authority to us given for that purpose, do by these presents, in the name and in behalf of our respective constituents, fully and entirely ratify and confirm each and every of the said articles of confederation and perpetual union, and all and singular the matters and things therein contained: And we do further solemnly plight and engage the faith of our respective constituents, that they shall abide by the determinations of the united states in congress assembled, on all questions, which by the said confederation are submitted to them. And that the articles thereof shall be inviolably observed by the states we respectively represent, and that the union shall be perpetual. In witness whereof we have hereunto set our hands in congress. Done at Philadelphia in the state of Pennsylvania the ninth Day of July in the Year of our Lord, one Thousand seven Hundred and Seventy eight, and in the third year of the Independence of America.

On the part of and behalf of the State of Newhampshire:
Josiah Bartlett
John Wentworth, junior; 8 August, 1778

On the part and behalf of the State of Rhodeisland and
      Providence Plantations:
William Ellery
Henry Marchant

John Collins

On the part and behalf of the State of New-York:
James Duane
Francis Lewis
William Duer
Gouvernour Morris

On the part and behalf of the State of Pennsylvania:
Robert Morris
Daniel Roberdeau
Jonathan Bayard Smith
William Clingan
Joseph Reed; 22 July, 1778

On the part and behalf of the State of Maryland:
John Hanson; 1 March, 1781
Daniel Carroll

On the part and behalf of the State of North-Carolina:
John Penn; 21 July, 1778
Cornelius Harnett
John Williams

On the part and behalf of the State of Georgia:
John Walton; 24 July, 1778
Edward Telfair
Edward Langworthy

On the part of and behalf of the State of Massachusetts-
        bay:
John Hancock
Samuel Adams
Elbridge Gerry
Francis Dana
James Lovell
Samuel Holten

On the part and behalf of the State of Connecticut:

Roger Sherman
Samuel Huntington
Oliver Wolcott
Titus Hosmer
Andrew Adams

On the Part and in Behalf of the State of New-Jersey, 26
    November, 1778:
John Witherspoon
Nathaniel Scudder

On the part and behalf of the State of Delaware:
Thomas McKean; 22 February, 1779
John Dickinson; 5 May, 1779
Nicholas Van Dyke

On the part and behalf of the State of Virginia:
Richard Henry Lee [Gen. Robert E. Lee's first cousin]
John Banister
Thomas Adams
John Harvie
Francis Lightfoot Lee [Gen. Robert E. Lee's first cousin]

On the part and behalf of the State of South-Carolina:
Henry Laurens
William Henry Drayton
John Mathews
Richard Hutson
Thomas Heyward, junior

EXPLANATION: By appending their names to the final page, representatives from the thirteen states both recognized and ratified the rules set forth in the Articles of Confederation. The "union," that is, the Constitution (the Articles themselves), is held to be "perpetual" (distinct from the "firm league of friendship"). The date is July 9, 1778. As is clear from the dates of many of the signatories, names were signed at varying periods of time, some, as with Maryland, as late as 1781.

Appendix

a position officially known as

"President of the United States in Congress Assembled"

(Notes: As specified in Article 9 of the Articles of Confederation each term was
limited to one year. Several men served partial terms, otherwise there would
have only been eight presidents. Debate continues as to whether these
individuals were true U.S. presidents or merely heads of Congress.)

1. **SAMUEL HUNTINGTON** of Connecticut (1731-1796): served from
   September 28, 1779, to July 6, 1781.

2. **THOMAS MCKEAN** of Delaware (1734-1817): served from July 10, 1781,
   to November 4, 1781.

3. **JOHN HANSON** of Maryland (1715-1783): served from November 5, 1781,
   to November 4, 1782.

4. **ELIAS BOUDINOT** of New Jersey (1740-1821): served from November 4,
   1782, to November 3, 1783.

5. **THOMAS MIFFLIN** of Pennsylvania (1744-1800): served from November
   3, 1783, to June 3, 1784.

6. **RICHARD HENRY LEE** of Virginia (1732-1794): served from November 30,
   1784, to November 23, 1785.

7. **JOHN HANCOCK** of Massachusetts (1737-1793): served from November
   23, 1785, to June 6, 1786.

8. **NATHANIEL GORHAM** of Massachusetts (1738-1796): served from June 6,
   1786, to November 13, 1786.

9. **ARTHUR ST. CLAIR** of Pennsylvania (1737-1818): served from February 2,
   1787, to October 29, 1787.

10. **CYRUS GRIFFIN** of Virginia (1748-1810): served from January 22, 1788,
    to March 4, 1789.

COURTEOUS
We are PROMPT
RELIABLE

SEA RAVEN PRESS

• WE ARE OPEN 24 HOURS A DAY, 7 DAYS A WEEK
• WE ARE ALWAYS STRIVING TO IMPROVE OUR SERVICE
• WE ARE CONSTANTLY WORKING ON NEW PRODUCTS
• WE ARE YOUR GO-TO SOURCE FOR AUTHENTIC HISTORY BOOKS
• WE ALSO PROVIDE ONE-OF-A-KIND MERCHANDISE FOR THE HOME

Unique Books and Gifts
For the Whole Family!

ALL OUR PRODUCTS PROUDLY MADE IN AMERICA
WE DELIVER ANYWHERE IN THE WORLD

SeaRavenPress.com

Bibliography
AND SUGGESTED READING

Adams, Charles. *When in the Course of Human Events: Arguing the Case for Southern Secession.* Lanham, MD: Rowman and Littlefield, 2000.

Adams, Henry (ed.). *Documents Relating to New-England Federalism, 1800-1815.* Boston, MA: Little, Brown, and Co., 1877.

Bateman, William O. *Political and Constitutional Law of the United States of America.* St. Louis: G. I. Jones and Co., 1876.

Bledsoe, Albert Taylor. *A Theodicy; or a Vindication of the Divine Glory, as Manifested in the Constitution and Government of the Moral World.* New York: Carlton and Porter, 1856.

Clare, Israel Smith. *Illustrated Universal History: Being a Clear and Concise History of All Nations.* Philadelphia: J. C. McCurdy and Co., 1881.

Collier, Christopher, and James Lincoln Collier. *Decision in Philadelphia: The Constitutional Convention of 1787.* 1986. New York: Ballantine, 1987 ed.

Desty, Robert. *The Constitution of the United States.* San Francisco: Sumner Whitney and Co., 1881.

Elliot, Jonathan. *The Debates in the Several State Conventions on the Adoption of the Federal Constitution, As Recommended by the General Convention at Philadelphia in 1787.* 5 vols. Philadelphia: J. B. Lippincott, 1861.

Findlay, Bruce, and Esther Findlay. *Your Rugged Constitution: How America's House of Freedom is Planned and Built.* 1950. Stanford, CA: Stanford University Press, 1951 ed.

Graham, John Remington. *A Constitutional History of Secession.* Gretna, LA: Pelican Publishing Co., 2003.

Harding, Samuel Bannister. *The Contest Over the Ratification of the Federal Constitution in the State of Massachusetts.* New York: Longmans, Green, and Co., 1896.

Hickey, William. *The Constitution of the United States.* Philadelphia: T. K. and P. G. Collins, 1853

Jensen, Merrill. *The New Nation: A History of the United States During the Confederation, 1781-1789.* New York: Vintage, 1950.

——. *The Articles of Confederation: An Interpretation of the Social-Constitutional History of the American Revolution, 1774-1781.* Madison, WI: University of Wisconsin Press, 1959.

Kelly, Alfred H., Winfred A. Harbison, and Herman Belz. *The American Constitution: Its Origins and Development* (Vol. 2). 1965. New York: W. W. Norton and Co., 1991 ed.

Locke, John. *Two Treatises of Government* (Mark Goldie, ed.). 1924. London, UK: Everyman, 1998 ed.

Main, Jackson Turner. *The Anti-Federalists: Critics of the Constitution, 1781-1788.* 1961. New York: W. W. Norton and Co., 1974 ed.

Napolitano, Andrew P. *The Constitution in Exile: How the Federal Government has Seized Power by Rewriting the Supreme Law of the Land.* Nashville: Nelson Current, 2006.

Rawle, William. *A View of the Constitution of the United States of America.* Philadelphia: Philip H. Nicklin, 1829.

Samuel, Bunford. *Secession and Constitutional Liberty.* 2 vols. New York: Neale Publishing, 1920.

Seabrook, Lochlainn. *Carnton Plantation Ghost Stories: True Tales of the Unexplained from Tennessee's Most Haunted Civil War House!* 2005. Franklin, TN, 2016 ed.

——. *Nathan Bedford Forrest: Southern Hero, American Patriot.* 2007. Franklin, TN, 2010 ed.

——. *Abraham Lincoln: The Southern View.* 2007. Franklin, TN: Sea Raven Press, 2013 ed.

——. *The McGavocks of Carnton Plantation: A Southern History - Celebrating One of Dixie's Most Noble Confederate Families and Their Tennessee Home.* 2008. Franklin, TN, 2011 ed.

——. *A Rebel Born: A Defense of Nathan Bedford Forrest.* 2010. Franklin, TN: Sea Raven Press, 2011 ed.

——. *A Rebel Born: The Screenplay* (for the film). 2011. Franklin, TN: Sea Raven Press.

——. *Everything You Were Taught About the Civil War is Wrong, Ask a Southerner!* 2010. Franklin, TN: Sea Raven Press, revised 2014 ed.

——. *The Quotable Jefferson Davis: Selections From the Writings and Speeches of the Confederacy's First President.* Franklin, TN: Sea Raven Press, 2011.

——. *The Quotable Robert E. Lee: Selections From the Writings and Speeches of the South's Most Beloved Civil War General.* Franklin, TN: Sea Raven Press, 2011 Sesquicentennial Civil War Edition.

——. *Lincolnology: The Real Abraham Lincoln Revealed In His Own Words.* Franklin, TN: Sea Raven Press, 2011.

——. *The Unquotable Abraham Lincoln: The President's Quotes They Don't Want You To Know!* Franklin, TN: Sea Raven Press, 2011.

——. *Honest Jeff and Dishonest Abe: A Southern Children's Guide to the Civil War.* Franklin, TN: Sea Raven Press, 2012.

——. *Encyclopedia of the Battle of Franklin - A Comprehensive Guide to the Conflict that Changed the Civil War.* Franklin, TN: Sea Raven Press, 2012.

——. *The Quotable Nathan Bedford Forrest: Selections From the Writings and Speeches of the Confederacy's Most Brilliant Cavalryman.* Spring Hill, TN: Sea Raven Press, 2012.

——. *Forrest! 99 Reasons to Love Nathan Bedford Forrest.* Spring Hill, TN: Sea Raven Press, 2012.

——. *Give 'Em Hell Boys! The Complete Military Correspondence of Nathan Bedford Forrest.* Spring Hill, TN: Sea Raven Press, 2012.

——. *The Constitution of the Confederate States of America Explained: A Clause-by-Clause Study of the South's Magna Carta.* Spring Hill, TN: Sea Raven Press, 2012 Sesquicentennial Civil War Edition.

——. *The Great Impersonator: 99 Reasons to Dislike Abraham Lincoln.* Spring Hill, TN: Sea Raven Press, 2012.

——. *The Old Rebel: Robert E. Lee As He Was Seen By His Contemporaries.* Spring Hill, TN: Sea Raven Press, 2012 Sesquicentennial Civil War Edition.

——. *The Quotable Stonewall Jackson: Selections From the Writings and Speeches of the South's Most Famous General.* Spring Hill, TN: Sea Raven Press, 2012 Sesquicentennial Civil War Edition.

——. *Saddle, Sword, and Gun: A Biography of Nathan Bedford Forrest for Teens.* Spring Hill, TN: Sea Raven Press, 2013.

——. *The Alexander H. Stephens Reader: Excerpts From the Works of a Confederate Founding Father.* Spring Hill, TN: Sea Raven Press, 2013.

——. *The Quotable Alexander H. Stephens: Selections From the Writings and Speeches of the Confederacy's First Vice President.* Spring Hill, TN: Sea Raven Press, 2013 Sesquicentennial Civil War Edition.

——. *Give This Book to a Yankee! A Southern Guide to the Civil War for Northerners.* Spring Hill, TN: Sea Raven Press, 2014.

——. *Confederate Blood and Treasure: An Interview With Lochlainn Seabrook.* Spring Hill, TN: Sea Raven Press, 2015.

——. *Nathan Bedford Forrest and the Battle of Fort Pillow: Yankee Myth, Confederate Fact.* Spring Hill, TN: Sea Raven Press, 2015.

——. *Everything You Were Taught About American Slavery War is Wrong, Ask a Southerner!* Spring Hill, TN: Sea Raven Press, 2015.

——. *Confederacy 101: Amazing Facts You Never Knew About America's Oldest Political Tradition.* Spring Hill, TN: Sea Raven Press, 2015.

——. *The Great Yankee Coverup: What the North Doesn't Want You to Know About Lincoln's War!* Spring Hill, TN: Sea Raven Press, 2015.

——. *Slavery 101: Amazing Facts You Never Knew About America's "Peculiar Institution."* Spring Hill, TN: Sea Raven Press, 2015.

——. *Confederate Flag Facts: What Every American Should Know About Dixie's Southern Cross.* Spring Hill, TN: Sea Raven Press, 2016.

——. *Nathan Bedford Forrest and the Ku Klux Klan: Yankee Myth, Confederate Fact.* Spring Hill, TN: Sea Raven Press, 2016.

——. *Seabrook's Bible Dictionary of Traditional and Mystical Christian Doctrines.* Spring Hill, TN: Sea Raven Press, 2016.

——. *Everything You Were Taught About African-Americans and the Civil War is Wrong, Ask a Southerner!* Spring Hill, TN: Sea Raven Press, 2016.

——. *Nathan Bedford Forrest and African-Americans: Yankee Myth, Confederate Fact.* Spring Hill, TN: Sea Raven Press, 2016.

——. *Women in Gray: A Tribute to the Ladies Who Supported the Southern Confederacy.* Spring Hill, TN: Sea Raven Press, 2016.

——. *Lincoln's War: The Real Cause, the Real Winner, the Real Loser.* Spring Hill, TN: Sea Raven Press, 2016.

——. *The Unholy Crusade: Lincoln's Legacy of Destruction in the American South.* Spring Hill, TN: Sea Raven Press, 2017.

——. *Abraham Lincoln Was a Liberal, Jefferson Davis Was a Conservative: The Missing Key to Understanding the American Civil War.* Spring Hill, TN: Sea Raven Press, 2017.

——. *All We Ask is to be Let Alone: The Southern Secession Fact Book.* Spring Hill, TN: Sea Raven Press, 2017.

——. *The Ultimate Civil War Quiz Book: How Much Do You Really Know About America's Most Misunderstood Conflict?* Spring Hill, TN: Sea Raven Press, 2017.

——. *Rise Up and Call Them Blessed: Victorian Tributes to the Confederate Soldier, 1861-1901.* Spring Hill, TN: Sea Raven Press, 2017.

——. *Victorian Confederate Poetry: The Southern Cause in Verse, 1861-1901.* Spring Hill, TN: Sea Raven Press, 2018.

——. *Confederate Monuments: Why Every American Should Honor Confederate Soldiers and Their Memorials.* Spring Hill, TN: Sea Raven Press, 2018.

——. *The God of War: Nathan Bedford Forrest as He Was Seen by His Contemporaries.* Spring Hill, TN: Sea Raven Press, 2018.

——. *I Rode With Forrest! Confederate Soldiers Who Served With the World's Greatest Cavalry Leader.* Spring Hill, TN: Sea Raven Press, 2018.

——. *The Battle of Spring Hill: Recollections of Confederate and Union Soldiers.* Spring Hill, TN: Sea Raven Press, 2018.

——. *The Battle of Franklin: Recollections of Confederate and Union Soldiers.* Spring Hill, TN: Sea Raven Press, 2018.

——. *The Battle of Nashville: Recollections of Confederate and Union Soldiers.* Spring Hill, TN: Sea Raven Press, 2018.

——. (ed.) *A Short History of the Confederate States of America* (Jefferson Davis, Belford Company, NY, 1890). A Sea Raven Press Reprint. Spring Hill, TN: Sea Raven Press, 2020.

——. (ed.) *Prison Life of Jefferson Davis: Embracing Details and Incidents in his Captivity, With Conversations on Topics of Public Interest* (John J. Craven, Sampson, Low, Son, and Marston, London, UK, 1866). A Sea Raven Press Reprint. Spring Hill, TN: Sea Raven Press, 2020.

——. *What the Confederate Flag Means to Me: Americans Speak Out in Defense of Southern Honor, Heritage, and History.* Spring Hill, TN: Sea Raven Press, 2021.

——. *Heroes of the Southern Confederacy: The Illustrated Book of Confederate Officials, Soldiers, and Civilians.* Spring Hill, TN: Sea Raven Press, 2021.

——. *Support Your Local Confederate: Wit and Humor in the Southern Confederacy.* Spring Hill, TN: Sea Raven Press, 2021.

——. *America's Three Constitutions: Complete Texts of the Articles of Confederation,*

Constitution of the United States of America, and Constitution of the Confederate States of America. Spring Hill, TN: Sea Raven Press, 2021.

——. *Vintage Southern Cookbook: 2,000 Delicious Dishes From Dixie.* Spring Hill, TN: Sea Raven Press, 2021.

Spaeth, Harold J., and Edward Conrad Smith. *The Constitution of the United States.* 1936. New York: HarperCollins, 1991 ed.

Swinton, William. *First Lessons in Our Country's History.* 1872. New York, NY: American Book Co., 1900 ed.

Upshur, Abel Parker. *A Brief Enquiry Into the True Nature and Character of Our Federal Government.* Philadelphia: John Campbell, 1863.

U.S. Congress. *The Constitutions of the Several Independent States of America; The Declaration of Independence; The Articles of Confederation Between the Said States; The Treaties Between His Most Christian Majesty and the United States of America.* Philadelphia: U.S. Congress, 1782.

Wallcut, R. F. (pub.). *Southern Hatred of the American Government, the People of the North, and Free Institutions.* Boston, MA: R. F. Wallcut, 1862.

"Books invite all; they constrain none."
Hartley Burr Alexander (1873-1939)

MEET THE AUTHOR

NEO-VICTORIAN SCHOLAR LOCHLAINN SEABROOK, a descendant of the families of Alexander Hamilton Stephens, John Singleton Mosby, Edmund Winchester Rucker, and William Giles Harding, is a 7th generation Kentuckian and the most prolific pro-South writer in the world today. Known by literary critics as the "new Shelby Foote" and by his fans as the "Voice of the Traditional South," he is a recipient of the prestigious Jefferson Davis Historical Gold Medal. As a lifelong writer he has authored and edited books ranging in topics from history, politics, science, religion, and biography, to nature, music, humor, gastronomy, and the paranormal; books that his readers describe as "game changers," "transformative," and "life altering."

One of the world's most popular living historians, he is a 17th generation Southerner of Appalachian heritage who descends from dozens of patriotic Revolutionary War soldiers and Confederate soldiers from Kentucky, Tennessee, North Carolina, and Virginia. A proud member of the Sons of the Confederate Veterans, he began life as a child prodigy, later transforming into a true Renaissance Man. Besides being an accomplished and well respected author-historian and Bible authority, he is also a Kentucky Colonel, eagle scout, screenwriter, nature, wildlife, and landscape photographer, artist, graphic designer, songwriter (3,000 songs), film composer, multi-instrument musician, vocalist, session player, music producer, genealogist, former history museum docent, and a former ranch hand, zookeeper, and wrangler.

His (currently) 77 adult and children's books contain some 60,000 well-researched pages that have earned him accolades from around the globe. His works, which have sold on every continent except Antarctica, have introduced hundreds of thousands to vital facts that have been left out of our mainstream books. He has been endorsed internationally by leading experts, museum curators, award-winning historians, bestselling authors, celebrities, filmmakers, noted scientists, well regarded educators, TV show hosts and producers, renowned military artists, esteemed heritage organizations, and distinguished academicians of all races, creeds, and colors. Colonel Seabrook holds the world record for writing the most books on Southern icon Nathan Bedford Forrest: 12.

Of northern, western, and central European ancestry, he is the 6th great-grandson of the Earl of Oxford and a descendant of European royalty. His modern day cousins include: Johnny Cash, Elvis Presley, Lisa Marie Presley, Billy Ray and Miley Cyrus, Patty Loveless, Tim McGraw, Lee Ann Womack, Dolly Parton, Pat Boone, Naomi, Wynonna, and Ashley Judd, Ricky Skaggs, the Sunshine Sisters, Martha Carson, Chet Atkins, Patrick J. Buchanan, Cindy Crawford, Bertram Thomas Combs (Kentucky's 50th governor), Edith Bolling (second wife of President Woodrow Wilson), Andy Griffith, Riley Keough, George C. Scott, Robert Duvall, Reese Witherspoon, Lee Marvin, Rebecca Gayheart, and Tom Cruise.

A constitutionalist and avid outdoorsman and gun advocate, Colonel Seabrook is the author of the international blockbuster, *Everything You Were Taught About the Civil War is Wrong, Ask a Southerner!* He lives with his wife and family in beautiful historic Middle Tennessee, the heart of the Confederacy.

If you enjoyed this book you will be interested in Colonel Seabrook's popular related titles:

☛ ABRAHAM LINCOLN WAS A LIBERAL, JEFFERSON DAVIS WAS A CONSERVATIVE
☛ EVERYTHING YOU WERE TAUGHT ABOUT THE CIVIL WAR IS WRONG, ASK A SOUTHERNER!
☛ ALL WE ASK IS TO BE LET ALONE: THE SOUTHERN SECESSION FACT BOOK
☛ EVERYTHING YOU WERE TAUGHT ABOUT AMERICAN SLAVERY IS WRONG, ASK A SOUTHERNER!
☛ CONFEDERATE FLAG FACTS: WHAT EVERY AMERICAN SHOULD KNOW ABOUT DIXIE'S SOUTHERN CROSS
☛ LINCOLN'S WAR: THE REAL CAUSE, THE REAL WINNER, THE REAL LOSER

Available from Sea Raven Press and wherever fine books are sold

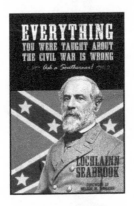
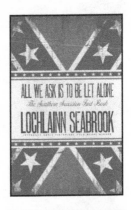

ALL OF OUR BOOK COVERS ARE AVAILABLE AS 11" X 17" COLOR POSTERS, SUITABLE FOR FRAMING

SeaRavenPress.com

CPSIA information can be obtained
at www.ICGtesting.com
Printed in the USA
LVHW010921211122
733504LV00005B/195